Writer's Toolbox

Picture Window Books
Minneapolis, Minnesota

Special thanks to our adviser, Terry Flaherty, Ph.D.,
Professor of English, Minnesota State University, Mankato,
for his expertise.

by
Nancy Loewen

illustrated by
Christopher Lyles,
Dawn Beacon, and
Todd Ouren

Learn How to Write

- Letters
- Fairy Tales
- Scary Stories
- Journals
- Poems
- Reports

TABLE OF CONTENTS

Once Upon a Time

Writing Your Own Fairy Tale

A goose lays golden eggs. A frog turns into a prince. A magic beanstalk grows high into the clouds—where a giant lives!

What kinds of stories are these? Fairy tales, of course.

Fairy tales are very old stories with magical characters. Every culture has its own fairy tales. When the stories formed, few people could read or write. The tales were spoken out loud.

Let's take a close look at the popular story "Little Red Riding Hood." You'll see how the right tools can help you write your own fairy tale!

Once upon a time, in a woods far away, lived a little girl. She owned a red cloak with a hood. She wore it all the time. Everyone called her Little Red Riding Hood.

~ Tool 1 ~

The **SETTING** is the time and place of a story. In fairy tales, the setting is made up. The stories happen in the distant past. The place might be an imaginary forest, village, or castle. No real time or place is described. The setting of "Little Red Riding Hood" is a faraway forest, long ago.

~ Tool 2 ~

The **CHARACTERS** are the people or creatures in the story. The main character is the one that appears most often in the story. In this fairy tale, Little Red Riding Hood is the main character.

~ Tool 3 ~

The **PLOT** is what happens in a story. In fairy tales, the plot moves quickly. We don't learn much about Little Red Riding Hood. We don't learn much about her mother or grandmother. Instead, the action begins right away.

One day, Little Red Riding Hood's mother gave her a basket. "Here are some cakes and breads," her mother told her. "Take them to your grandmother. She is ill. The treats will give her strength."

As Little Red Riding Hood set off, her mother called after her. "Stay on the path!" she said. "Don't stop to play along the way!"

~ Tool 4 ~

DIALOGUE is what characters say to each other. Good dialogue helps move the story along. It gives the reader information.

~ Tool 5 ~

In fairy tales, characters often get **WARNINGS**, like the one given here by Little Red Riding Hood's mother. Warnings give the reader clues about what might happen later in the story.

"I'll be careful," the girl said.

Little Red Riding Hood walked deeper and deeper into the woods. After a while, she met a wolf. She didn't know that the wolf was a wicked creature, so she wasn't the least bit scared.

~ Tool 6 ~

All fairy tales contain **MAGIC.** That's one of the things that sets them apart from other old stories. Fairy tales can be about witches, giants, trolls, elves, and animals. They can be about kings and queens, princes and princesses. Objects, such as mirrors and clocks, can come to life. And, yes, fairy tales can be about fairies, too!

"Good morning," said the wolf. "Where are you off to on this fine day?"

"I'm bringing this basket of cakes and breads to my grandmother," Little Red Riding Hood explained. "She is ill, and these treats will give her strength."

"Where does your grandmother live?" the wolf asked.

"She lives in a small wooden house farther up the path," Little Red Riding Hood said.

~ Tool 7 ~

Fairy tales often have characters who are filled with **GREED**. These characters want something that someone else has. And they will do anything to get it. Here the wolf wants an extra-big lunch. That means there's trouble ahead for Little Red Riding Hood!

The wicked wolf was very hungry. He wanted to eat both the girl and her grandmother for lunch. Quickly he thought of an evil plan.

~ Tool 8 ~

In fairy tales, characters often use **TRICKS** to fool each another. Little Red Riding Hood wants to do the right thing. But the wolf gets her thinking about the flowers. She ignores her mother's warnings and runs off to the field. The wolf's plan works perfectly.

"Your grandmother might like some flowers, too," the wolf suggested. He pointed to a clearing in the woods. "Look at that field. It has flowers of every color!"

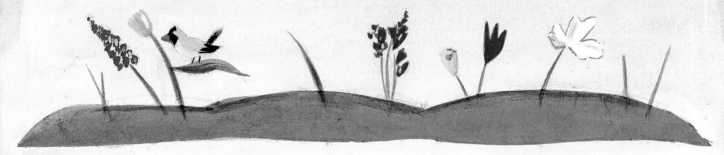

"But Mother told me to stay on the path and not to stop," Little Red Riding Hood said.

"Nonsense!" the wolf said. "It will take just a minute. The flowers will cheer up your grandmother."

Little Red Riding Hood nodded. Her feet started edging off the path. "Yes," she said. "Yes, they will!" And she ran to gather flowers for her grandmother.

The evil wolf dashed off to the grandmother's house. He swallowed the poor woman whole! Then he put on her bonnet, got into her bed, and waited.

Before long, Little Red Riding Hood came skipping up the path. The front door was open, so she went right in.

"Hello! Grandmother!" she called. "I've brought you a basket of treats, and some flowers, too!"

~ Tool 9 ~

In many good fairy tales, the reader knows a **SECRET**—something the characters don't. Little Red Riding Hood has no idea that the wolf is in her grandmother's bed. But you do!

Little Red Riding Hood became uneasy when
she looked at her grandmother.

"Grandmother," she said slowly.
"What big ears you have."

"The better to hear you with, my child,"
    the wolf said.

"Grandmother, what big eyes you have."

"The better to see you with, my sweet."

The **REPETITION** of words or actions gives them more power. Using nearly the same words, Little Red Riding Hood notices the wolf's ears ... then eyes ... then teeth. The suspense builds. When the wolf jumps out of bed, the little girl is frightened, and so are we!

"And Grandmother, what big teeth you have!"

"The better to EAT you with!"
the wolf snarled. He jumped out of bed
and swallowed poor
Little Red Riding
Hood, too.

With his stomach filled,
the wolf lay back down
for a nap. He snored loudly.

Z Z Z Z

A hunter passed by.
He knew the old woman
and was puzzled by the snoring.
She couldn't possibly be so loud.
He went into the house and
found the wolf.

He raised his gun.

~ Tool 11 ~

In fairy tales, greedy characters often make **MISTAKES**. These mistakes then lead to their downfall. What if the wolf hadn't taken a nap?

Then the hunter noticed the wolf's big belly. He put down his gun, took out a pair of scissors, and cut open the wolf's stomach.

Out jumped Little Red Riding Hood. And out crawled the old grandmother.

~ Tool 12 ~

In some fairy tales, **PROBLEM-SOLVING** happens through luck or magic. That's what happens in this story. The hunter comes along at just the right time and stops the evil wolf. Little Red Riding Hood and her grandmother get out of trouble through luck.

In other fairy tales, characters get out of trouble on their own. They solve their problem by being brave, strong, or clever.

The three quickly filled
the wolf's stomach with
stones and sewed him
back up. The wolf awoke
and tried to run away.
But he was too heavy
to move!

He fell to the
floor, dead.

The hunter went home with the dead wolf's skin.
The grandmother ate her treats and soon became well.

~ Tool 13 ~

Fairy tales come to a **PLEASING END.** They sometimes close with "And they lived happily ever after." The reader is left with the idea that nothing bad will happen to those characters ever again.

And Little Red Riding Hood promised that she would always listen to her mother and stay on the path!

THE END

Let's Review!

These are the **13 tools** you need to write great fairy tales.

Fairy tales take place in made-up times and places, or SETTINGS **(1)**. They usually begin, "Once upon a time" and have good and bad CHARACTERS **(2)**. A fairy tale PLOT **(3)** moves quickly. Actions are more important than details. DIALOGUE **(4)** between characters often includes WARNINGS **(5)**.

Fairy tales include MAGIC **(6)**. A wolf blows down a house made of sticks. A gingerbread cookie comes to life. A fairy godmother turns mice into horses.

The bad characters in a fairy tale are often filled with GREED **(7)**. They use TRICKS **(8)** to get what they want.

The reader often knows a SECRET **(9)**, information the characters don't. The REPETITION **(10)** of words or actions can build suspense.

Bad characters usually make MISTAKES **(11)** that lead to their downfall. Good characters SOLVE THEIR PROBLEM **(12)** on their own, or through luck or magic, bringing the fairy tale to a PLEASING END **(13)**.

Getting Started Exercises

✏➤ Look at the objects around you. Pick one. What if that object came to life? What would it do? What might it want? What special powers would it have?

✏➤ Pick one or two words from each of the following lists. What does each word make you think of? Let those thoughts be the starting point of your story.

- queen, king, scarecrow, boy, girl, frog, butterfly, jellyfish, gorilla
- marry, bake, chatter, dig, hop, hum, twist, gobble, poke, dance
- lake, palace, seed, spoon, ticket, riddle, rope, quicksand, peach
- skinny, smart, pink, fearful, lazy, windy, juicy, nervous, quick

✏➤ Think of something you like, and play a "what if" game. Let's say your choice is ice cream. What if people ate ice cream all day long? What if someone stole all the ice cream in the world? What if ice cream gave people special powers? Play around with your ideas, and pretty soon you'll have a story!

Writing Tips

 Fairy tales don't have a lot of details. But the details that are there are very important. Here's an example from "Little Red Riding Hood." After swallowing both Little Red Riding Hood and her grandmother, the wolf takes a nap. He snores loudly—so loudly that the hunter hears him! That one detail affects the whole story.

 Have your characters talk to each other. Good dialogue gives life to your characters.

 Fairy tales are about feelings that we all have. Think about what your characters are doing. Are they feeling love, courage, joy, anger, or fear? Your story will be stronger if your characters have strong feelings.

Sincerely Yours

Writing Your Own Letter

Dear Reader,

Suppose you lived 200 years ago. You needed to get a message to your cousin Jane, who lived many miles away. You couldn't call Jane on your telephone, because phones hadn't been invented yet. You couldn't e-mail her. You couldn't send her a text message. How would you contact Jane?

You would write her a letter, of course!

A letter is a written message from one person (or group) to another. For hundreds of years, letters were the only way for people in distant places to communicate with each other.

Today we can communicate in lots of ways, but letters are still important. We read or write letters nearly every day—at work, at play, and everywhere in between.

To learn more about letters, keep reading!

Sincerely,

Nancy Loewen

Nancy Loewen
Author

Most of the letters we write fall into two groups: business and friendly. We write business letters to people we don't know, so it's important to follow the rules. We write friendly letters to people we know well, so we can be less formal.

Most letters have five basic parts: heading, greeting, body, closing, and signature/signature line. We'll be using these terms in the pages ahead, so take a good look at the following example.

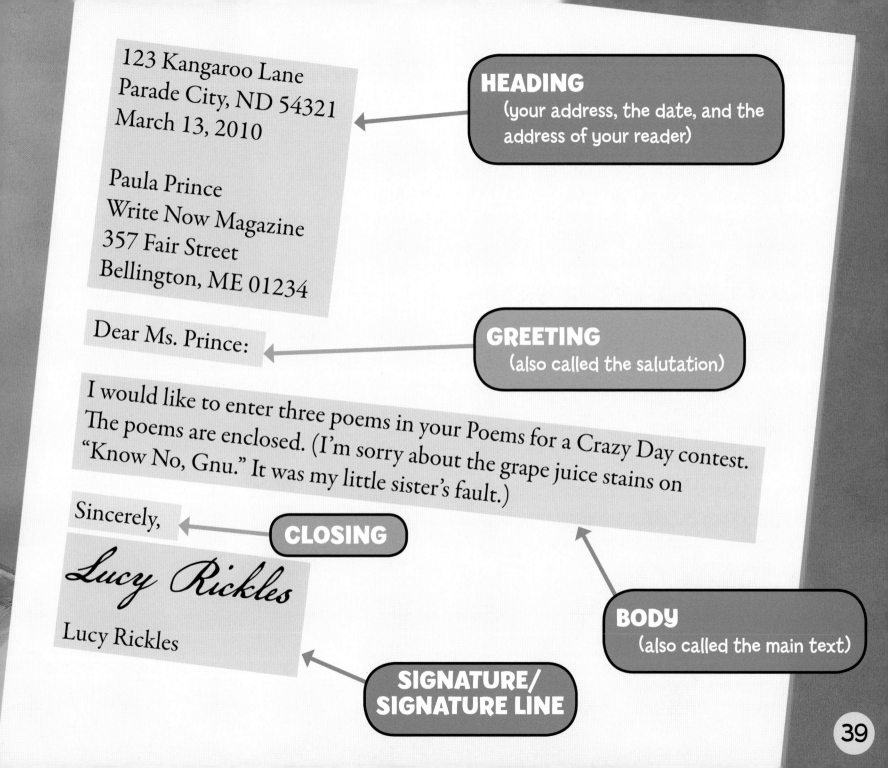

123 Kangaroo Lane
Parade City, ND 54321
March 13, 2010

Paula Prince
Write Now Magazine
357 Fair Street
Bellington, ME 01234

HEADING
(your address, the date, and the address of your reader)

Dear Ms. Prince:

GREETING
(also called the salutation)

I would like to enter three poems in your Poems for a Crazy Day contest. The poems are enclosed. (I'm sorry about the grape juice stains on "Know No, Gnu." It was my little sister's fault.)

BODY
(also called the main text)

Sincerely,

CLOSING

Lucy Rickles

Lucy Rickles

SIGNATURE/ SIGNATURE LINE

Let's get started by learning how to write a friendly letter.

~ Tool 1 ~

In a friendly letter, the **HEADING** has two parts: your address and the date. However, if you're writing to a really close friend or family member, you don't need to include your address. In that case, all you need is the date.

~ Tool 2 ~

The most common **GREETING** is "Dear," with the name followed by a comma. But if you know the reader really well, you can open your letter however you want. Sound like yourself!

Hey, Joe!
Yo, Joe.
Hi,
Dude!

3 Gray Duck Row
Bunnydale, KY 44444
March 27, 2010

Dear Joe,

~ Tool 3 ~

The **BODY** of a friendly letter should sound like you're talking. You can write about the things that are happening in your life. You should also show that you're interested in the other person's life. Ask questions, and you'll be more likely to get a letter back in return.

3 Gray Duck Row
Bunnydale, KY 44444
March 27, 2010

Dear Joe,

Guess what? I'm coming to see you! My parents say we can spend a few days in Chicago on our summer vacation. I can't wait.

How is your new school? Have you made some new friends? Everyone in Mr. Glidden's class really misses you.

Your tater-tot-tower record still stands. Mike tried to break it yesterday, but the tater tots fell down when he burped.

Write back soon!

~ Tool 4 ~

There are lots of ways to close a friendly letter. "Your friend," "Take care," and "Love" are some common **CLOSINGS.** But feel free to make up your own!

All my love,
Hugs and kisses,
Later, dude!
See you soon,
Thinking of you,

~ Tool 5 ~

The **SIGNATURE** is your handwritten name. If you're writing to a really close friend or family member, use just your first name.

3 Gray Duck Row
Bunnydale, KY 44444
March 27, 2010

Dear Joe,

Guess what? I'm coming to see you! My parents say we can spend a few days in Chicago on our summer vacation. I can't wait.

How is your new school? Have you made some new friends? Everyone in Mr. Glidden's class really misses you.

Your tater-tot-tower reco_____ ___ke tried to break it yesterday, but the tater tots fell d___

Write back soon!

Your friend,

Sam

Often, friendly letters are just about staying in touch. But we also use friendly letters to show our feelings about special situations.

Thank you notes are friendly letters, too. So are get well cards. These letters don't need to be long. But you should include a few details to show your reader that you've put some thought into it.

Dear Brad,

Thank you for coming to my birthday party. It was great to see you. Thanks for the metal detector, too. I've already found two quarters, an old pop can, and something else I can't identify. I can't wait to see what I find next!

Thanks again,

Zach

~ Tool 6 ~

PROOFREADING is important no matter what kind of letter you're writing. Pay attention to your spelling, punctuation, and grammar. A sloppy letter tells the reader that you were in a hurry, or that you didn't care.

Dear Amanda,

I'm sorry you broke your leg. That must have hurt! It's too bad you had to miss your hockey tournament. I hope you feel better soon.

Love,

Margie

49

~ Tool 7 ~

After you've finished your letter, you might remember something else you wanted to say. Do you have to start all over? No! A **POSTSCRIPT** is a sentence or short paragraph added to the end of a letter, after the signature. Use the initials *P.S.*, and then add what you want.

Dear Amanda,

I'm sorry you broke your leg. That must have hurt! It's too bad you had to miss your hockey tournament. I hope you feel better soon.

Love,

Margie

P.S. Can I sign your cast?

Now, let's move on to business letters!

ALFALFA AVE

~ Tool 1 ~

In a business letter, the **HEADING** has three parts: your address, the date, and the name and address of your reader.

101 Clover Lane
Mudville, WA 99999
October 6, 2010

Norah Brown
101 Alfalfa Avenue
Splashville, ID 88888

~ Tool 2 ~

The **GREETING** of a business letter usually begins with "Dear." If you're writing to a man, use "Mr." If you're writing to a woman, use "Ms." If you know the woman is married, you can use "Mrs." Then add the person's last name and a colon.

What if you don't know the person's name? Use one of these greetings:

> Dear Sir:
> Dear Madam:
> Dear Sir or Madam:
> To Whom It May Concern:

101 Clover Lane
Mudville, WA 99999
October 6, 2010

Norah Brown
101 Alfalfa Avenue
Splashville, ID 88888

Dear Ms. Brown:

~ Tool 3 ~

The **BODY** of a business letter should be polite and to the point. If you are asking the reader to do something, be sure to include all the information he or she will need.

In the letter on the opposite page, the writer states who she is. She explains how she heard of Ms. Brown. She quickly comes to the point of her letter, which is to ask for an interview. She gives her dad's name and phone number. And she does all of this in a very polite way.

101 Clover Lane
Mudville, WA 99999
October 6, 2010

Norah Brown
101 Alfalfa Avenue
Splashville, ID 88888

Dear Ms. Brown:

My name is Susan, and I'm in fourth grade at Grainwood Elementary. I read in the newspaper that you raise goats. Last month you won an award for your homemade goat cheese. Congratulations!

I am researching goats. May I talk to you about my project? Please call my father, Jeff, if you would like to set up an interview. Our number is 555-879-2241.

Thank you!

~ Tool 4 ~

"Sincerely" is a good **CLOSING** for a business letter. The word *sincerely* means "honestly and truthfully." But there are many other ways to close a business letter. Any of these closings would work:

Best wishes,
Cordially,
Regards,
With warm wishes,
Respectfully,

~ Tool 5 ~

The **SIGNATURE LINE** appears below your signature. It is simply your name. Use your first and last name. If you want, you can use your middle name, too.

If you are writing your business letter by hand, you should still include a signature line. Print your name, then sign above it.

Norah Brown
101 Alfalfa Avenue
Splashville, ID 88888

Dear Ms. Brown:

My name is Susan, and I'm in fourth grade at Grainwood Elementary. I read in the newspaper that you raise goats. Last month you won an award for your homemade goat cheese. Congratulations!

I am researching goats. May I talk to you about my project? Please call my father, Jeff, if you would like to set up an interview. Our number is 555-879-2241.

Thank you!

Sincerely,

Susan Fairfield

Susan Fairfield

~ Tool 8 ~

If you're sending a letter in the mail, you'll need to address an **ENVELOPE**.

Your name and address go in the upper left corner. This is called the return address. If your letter can't be delivered, it will be returned to you.

Your reader's name and address go in the middle of the envelope.

The stamp goes in the upper right corner.

Susan Fairfield
101 Clover Lane
Mudville, WA 99999

Norah Brown
101 Alfalfa Avenue
Splashville, ID 88888

Today, it's common to send e-mails instead of paper letters.

In e-mails, you can skip the heading. (The date is already in the e-mail, and you don't need the address.) But if you're writing someone you don't know, you should use a formal greeting and closing. Be respectful. And don't hit SEND until you've looked over your letter and fixed any mistakes.

Let's Review!

These are the **8 tools** you need to write great letters.

The **HEADING (1)** answers the questions Who, Where, and When. In a friendly letter, the heading has two parts. In a business letter, it has three.

The **GREETING (2)** is a polite way to get started. It's like saying "hello."

The **BODY (3)** answers the questions What and Why. The body gives your reason for writing. In a business letter, the body should be to the point. If you are asking for something, be sure to give the reader all the information he or she will need to help you.

The **CLOSING (4)** lets your reader know that you're almost done. Like the greeting, it's a way of being polite. The **SIGNATURE** and **SIGNATURE LINE (5)** let the reader know who wrote the letter.

PROOFREADING (6) helps you catch spelling and grammar mistakes.

The initials *P.S.* stand for **POSTSCRIPT (7)**. They bring attention to the fact that you're adding something to the letter.

Addressing the **ENVELOPE (8)** correctly is very important. You don't want your terrific letter to get lost in the mail!

Getting Started Exercises

- Pick out two characters in a favorite book. Pretend you are those characters, and have them write to each other about a problem they face in the story. What sorts of words would they use?

- Ask your parents or teachers if you can take part in a pen-pal program. You can make friends all around the world.

- Join a fan club, and write a letter to your favorite celebrity. Maybe you'll get a letter back!

- Do you feel strongly about something that's happening in your school? Write a letter to a school board member, and explain your thoughts.

Writing Tips

 Think of a letter as a little bit of YOU, going out into the world. The way you write should show how you would act if the person were right beside you. Would you hug that person or shake hands? Would you shout and laugh or would you use a quieter voice? Would you make jokes or talk politely?

 If you're writing a letter by hand, write a practice one first. When you're happy with what you've written, take a new piece of paper and rewrite the letter neatly.

 Have someone else look at your letter before you send it. Other people might see mistakes that you didn't notice.

 The best way to get really good at writing letters is to practice! You can write to your faraway friends and family. You can even write to people you see every day.

WORDS, WIT, AND WONDER

Writing Your Own Poem

Poetry is all around. It's in the nursery rhymes we learn when we're very young. It's in the songs we sing and the books we read.

Poetry ...

Plays with words and plants ideas ...
Opens our eyes and our
Ears ...
Twirls words into
Riddles, ribbons, and raindrops, and makes us say ...
Yes!

—Nancy Loewen

How are poems different from other kinds of writing?

For one thing, poems are usually written in short lines. They often rhyme, or have a set rhythm. Poems connect with our feelings and imaginations.

Poems can be funny or serious. They can tell a story or a joke. Or they might simply show us things from everyday life.

Let's take a look at some of the tools that poets use to create their work.

RHYTHM is important in music, and it's important in poetry, too. Think of every syllable as a beat—a tap on a drum. Some drumbeats are hard and loud. Some are soft. Together, the hard and soft beats form a pattern.

To hear rhythm in action, read the poem on the opposite page out loud. In the first line, say the words *was*, *Man*, and *beard* louder than the others. In the second line, say the words *said*, *just*, and *feared* louder. The pattern you hear is the poem's rhythm!

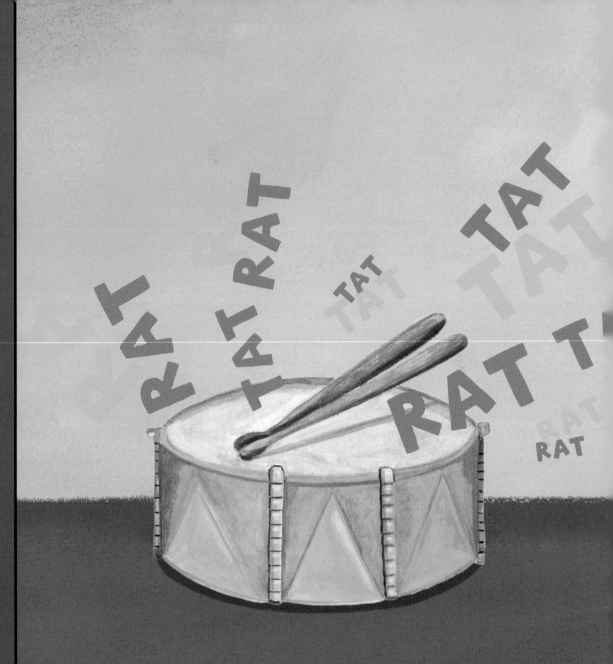

There was an Old Man with a beard,
Who said, "It is just as I feared!
Two Owls and a Hen,
Four Larks and a Wren,
Have all built their nests in my beard!"

—Edward Lear

~ Tool 2 ~

RHYME is often used to create rhythm. Rhyming words end with the same sound, like *cat* and *rat*, or *please* and *breeze*. In rhyming poems, the rhyming words come at the ends of lines.

In "Firefly," the words *by* and *sky* rhyme. So do *it* and *lit*. See how *wings* is repeated at the end of the third and sixth lines? It's not a rhyme, since it's the same word. But repeating the word works the same as a rhyme, and it brings the poem to a good close.

Firefly

A little light is going by,
Is going up to see the sky,
A little light with wings.

I never could have thought of it,

To have a little bug all lit

And made to go on wings.

—Elizabeth Madox Roberts

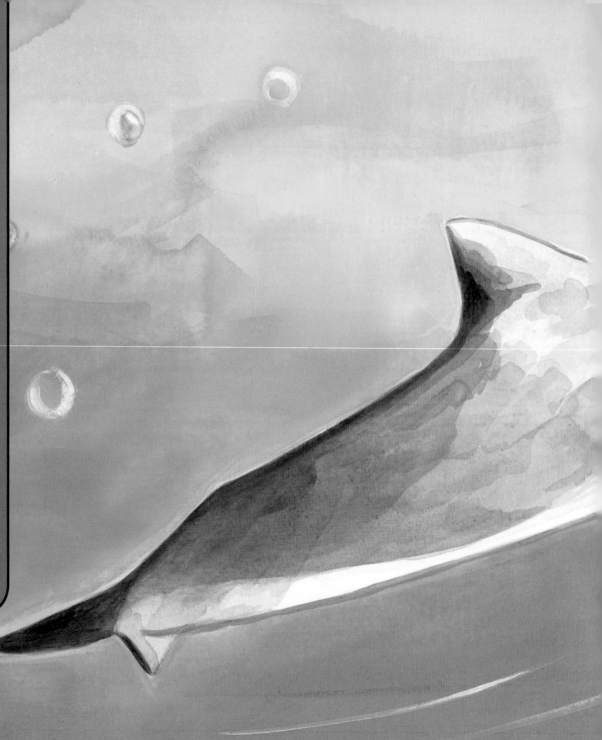

In rhyming poems, the rhythm is easy to see. But rhythm is important in poetry even if the words don't rhyme.

Look at the first two lines of "Sea Ribbons." The first line is long, with many hard and soft syllables. We spend some time reading it. We see the dolphin, and it seems to float in mid-air in front of us. The next line is very short. With three quick beats, we're plunging back into the water! The rhythm of each line matches what's happening in the poem.

Sea Ribbons

A dolphin soars into sparkling air and then
dives straight down
trailing a ribbon of silver bubbles that
echo her path, plunging,
spinning and funneling.

Racing up toward the sun, she
gathers speed for another joyous leap.

—Laura Purdie Salas

Piano

glossy black keys
clear white keys

step and rise
march in time

pairing up, sharing sounds
making music

—Laura Purdie Salas

As we saw earlier, rhyming poems often rhyme at the ends of lines. But rhyme can happen inside poems, too. And sometimes words don't rhyme exactly, but are alike enough to create a nice sound.

In "Piano," *rise* and *time* don't rhyme, but they come close. *Pairing* and *sharing* do rhyme, but they are inside the poem instead of at the ends of lines.

~ Tool 3 ~

In **ALLITERATION,** words start with the same letter sound.

Look at lines 3 to 6 of "Going to St. Ives." How many words start with an *s*? How many start with a *c* or *k*? Those are examples of alliteration.

Repeating letter sounds—no matter where they are in a word—makes a poem more fun to read. The words don't have to be right next to each other, but they should be nearby.

Going to St. Ives

1 As I was going to St. Ives

2 I met a man with seven wives.

3 Every wife had seven sacks,

4 Every sack had seven cats,

5 Every cat had seven kits.

6 Kits, cats, sacks, and wives,

7 How many were going to St. Ives?

~ Tool 4 ~

Sometimes, the best way to describe something is to compare it to something else. We can compare things using the words *like* or *as*. These comparisons are called **SIMILES**. For example, "It's as hot *as* an oven out there."

In the last four lines of "Fog," water is compared to curtains. This is a simile, because the word *like* is used.

Fog

Why is water as water
liquid diamonds
slices of brilliance

But water as fog
like pale theater curtains
opening inches before
your nose

—Laura Purdie Salas

~ Tool 5 ~

We can compare things without using any connecting words, too. We say something is something else. These comparisons are called **METAPHORS.** For example, "It's an oven out there."

In the first three lines of "Fog," water is compared to diamonds. This is a metaphor. Water isn't *like* liquid diamonds. It *is* liquid diamonds.

Words that sound like what they mean are examples of **ONOMATOPOEIA**. These words can add interest and fun to a poem. *Swish, click, boom, hiccup, honk,* and *buzz* are all examples of onomatopoeia.

Beep!
Splash!
Cock-a-doodle-doo!

Free!

We are popcorn kernels
In class, waiting for the bell
Ready to explode
Full of heat, vibrating with energy

RRRIIIIIIIINNNNNNNNNNNNNNNG!

We
POP
POP
POP

Out the doorway

Burst into the street

Fill the quiet with noise and motion

—Laura Purdie Salas

The poem "Free!" uses onomatopoeia. The words *ring* and *pop* sound like what they mean.

Free!

We are popcorn kernels
In class, waiting for the bell
Ready to explode
Full of heat, vibrating with energy

RRRIIIIIIINNNNNNNNNNNNNNNG!

We
POP
Pop
POP

Out the doorway
Burst into the street
Fill the quiet with noise and motion

—Laura Purdie Salas

"Free!" also gives us another example of using metaphor in poetry. Are kids in school really popcorn kernels? No—but they are alike in some ways. They both bounce with energy when they are set free. And in this case, the metaphor isn't limited to just a line or two. It's spread throughout the entire poem.

See how the extra space around the word *pop* makes it look like popcorn is flying across the page? The way words are laid out on the page is another way that poets add meaning to their work.

~ Tool 7 ~

The shape, or form, a poem takes is also a kind of tool poets use. An **ACROSTIC** is a bit like a puzzle. From top to bottom, the first letters of each line spell a word. But it's not just any word—it's the subject of the poem.

Here the first letters spell "spelling test," and the poem is about taking a spelling test.

The poem back on page 67 is an acrostic, too!

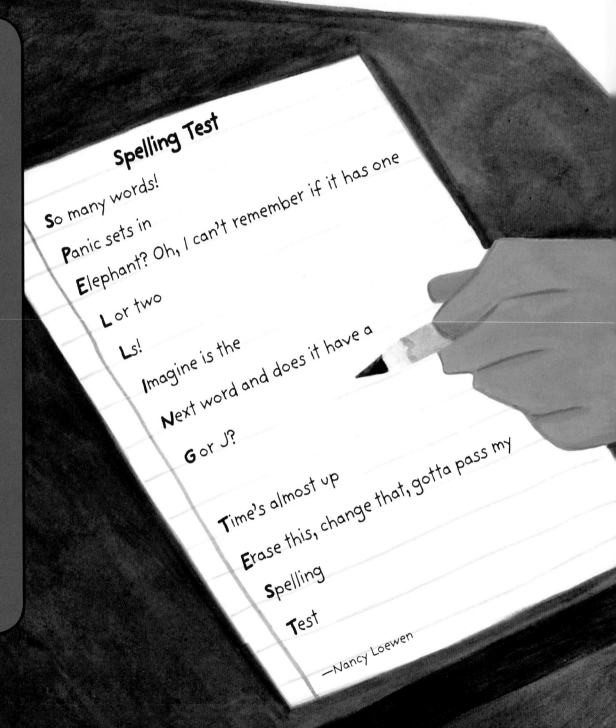

Spelling Test

So many words!

Panic sets in

Elephant? Oh, I can't remember if it has one

L or two

Ls!

Imagine is the

Next word and does it have a

G or J?

Time's almost up

Erase this, change that, gotta pass my

Spelling

Test

—Nancy Loewen

In Grandma's Barn

1 Kitten

2 Tiny nose, ears

3 Like snippets of soft felt

4 Eyes that will soon open for the

5 First time

—Nancy Loewen

~ Tool 9 ~

A **CONCRETE POEM** is a combination of poetry and art. These poems take the shape of their subjects. The actual words are still important—but so are what the words look like on the page.

The poem here is about a donut, and it looks like one, too!

I'll Take the One with Sprinkles, Please

SUGARY
YUM BRIGHT
FUN HAPPY CHEERFUL
SUGARY YUM BRIGHT FUN
HAPPY CHEERFUL SUGARY YUM
BRIGHT FUN HAPPY
CHEERFUL SUGARY
YUM HAPPY BRIGHT FUN
HAPPY CHEERFUL
SUGARY YUM BRIGHT
FUN HAPPY CHEERFUL
SUGARY YUMBRIGHT
FUN YUM HAPPY
CHEERFUL SUGARY
YUM BRIGHT FUN HAPPY
CHEERFUL SUGARY YUM BRIGHT
FUN HAPPY CHEERFUL
SUGARY YUM BRIGHT
FUN HAPPY

The Capitol: More Than Just a Building

It's not the building that makes us strong
It's not the flag that promises freedom

Behind that flag
Inside that building

People like me
People like you

We make the Capitol
We make our country

—Laura Purdie Salas

~ Tool 10 ~

FREE VERSE POEMS don't rhyme. They don't have a set number of syllables or lines, either. The ideas in the poem help the poet decide how to write it.

We've already seen four free verse poems in this book: "Sea Ribbons" on page 75, "Piano" on page 76, "Fog" on page 81, and "Free!" on page 83.

~ Tool 11 ~

HAIKU is a very old kind of poetry from Japan. A haiku is usually about nature, especially the seasons. It shows us a picture, but it doesn't include many details. Readers are left feeling they have discovered something.

Haiku usually don't have titles. They are made up of three lines, with syllables arranged like this:

Line one: 5 syllables
Line two: 7 syllables
Line three: 5 syllables

1 Footprints in deep snow

2 Suddenly, the sweep of wings

3 An unknown angel

—Nancy Loewen

There was a Young Lady whose eyes,
Were unique as to color and size;
When she opened them wide,
People all turned aside,
And started away in surprise.

—Edward Lear

~ Tool 12 ~

A **LIMERICK** is a short, silly rhyming poem. It was named after the county of Limerick in Ireland.

Limericks have five lines. The first two lines rhyme with the last line. Here, for example, *eyes* and *size* rhyme with *surprise*. The third and fourth lines are shorter, and rhyme with each other—in this case, *wide* and *aside*.

The poem back on page 71 is a limerick, too!

Let's Review!

These are the **12 tools** you need to write great poetry.

In poetry, every word must be chosen carefully. Poets choose words not only for their meaning, but also for sound and RHYTHM **(1)**.

RHYME **(2)** often takes place at the ends of lines. But rhyming words might be used within lines, too. ALLITERATION **(3)** can add interest to a poem by repeating letter sounds.

Poems often compare one thing to another in an imaginative way. To do this, they may use SIMILES **(4)** or METAPHORS **(5)**.

ONOMATOPOEIA **(6)** can make a poem fun to read and fun to hear.

Some poetic forms have rules. They must rhyme a certain way or have a set number of syllables per line. Other forms don't have any rules at all. The poetic forms discussed in this book are: ACROSTIC **(7)**, CINQUAIN **(8)**, CONCRETE **(9)**, FREE VERSE **(10)**, HAIKU **(11)**, and LIMERICK **(12)**.

Getting Started Exercises

- Write an acrostic with your friends or classmates. Pick a word and write it on a piece of paper, going downward. Pass it around, letting every person add a line to the poem.

- Practice using similes and metaphors. Pick an object and describe it. Go into a lot of detail—but don't name the object. Now, give the list to a friend or two. Have them guess what you're describing. Did they think you were writing about something else? If so, do you see how different things can share some of the same qualities? Maybe you've got the start of a poem!

- Put together a poetry reading! Get your classmates together and listen to each other's work. If you want, you can pick a subject. Maybe all the poems should be about music, sports, or winter. Or pick a specific form, such as haiku or cinquain.

Writing Tips

Keep a writing journal. As you go through your day, jot down the little things that you notice. Maybe the sky was pink this morning, or you saw a strange bird at the feeder. Maybe your baby sister said something that made you laugh. Your notes might someday become part of a poem.

Read your poetry out loud. (Record yourself, if possible.) Does it sound right? If you stumble over words, or the rhythm doesn't sound right, you might want to revise your work. (Revision is a big part of the writing process. Professional writers often revise their work many times.)

Find some poems you really like, and memorize them. The poems will be like good friends—always there when you need them.

If you're having trouble finishing a poem, put it away for a few days or weeks. When you come back to it, you might find that you know right away how to fix it.

It's All About You

Writing Your Own Journal

Imagine a place where you can say whatever you want. Whatever! And you can say it however you want.

There IS such a place. It's inside the pages of your very own journal.

A journal is a written record of your thoughts, feelings, and experiences. It's just for you—no one else should read it without your permission. A journal can take many forms: a blank book from a bookstore, a notebook, a file on a computer. The choice is yours!

Riley is a boy in the fourth grade. Let's take a peek inside his journal to learn more about how you can keep your own journal.

March 1

The new neighbors across the street moved in today. Huge truck. They unloaded all day. Tons of boxes. Looks like there are four kids. I think the two older ones will go to my school. Not sure. They have a chunky little dog with floppy ears. His name's Bugle. They have a purple and green snowmobeel, too. Cool!

~ Tool 1 ~

In a journal, you can record your **OBSERVATIONS**—the things that you see. It might be a strange cloud or a colorful bug on the sidewalk. It might be your friend making a funny face. Whatever it is, writing about it will help you remember it.

Notice that Riley doesn't always write in complete sentences. Sometimes he spells words wrong. That's OK. Riley's journal is just for him.

~ Tool 2 ~

A journal is a good place to write down your **EMOTIONS**. It doesn't matter what those emotions are—sadness, anger, fear, excitement, happiness. Riley didn't play well today and is feeling really bad. Writing in a journal can be like talking to a good friend.

March 8

I tried out for the traveling baseball team today. Really worried I didn't make it. I dropped a fly ball and only got a couple good hits. Mr. Franklin was there taking notes. When we were leaving, he smiled at Dan, but he didn't smile at me. I'm feeling pretty bad right now.

March 10

Didn't make the traveling team. Dan made it. I can't believe it. I thought I did better than he did. And now I'm grounded because my sister says I pushed her. I barely touched her. It's not my fault she's so clumsy.

LIFE ISN'T FAIR!!!

March 13

Today I found out I'm on the in-house baseball team with Xavier and Jeff! I always have fun with them. I'm feeling better now. I just want to get out and play. Can't wait for practice tomorrow.

~ Tool 3 ~

If writing in a journal is a school assignment, you might be asked to use **WRITING PROMPTS.** Prompts are directions that help get your writing mind going. They're a great way to get started if you can't think of anything to write about.

March 27

What is your favorite part of the weekend?

My favorite part of the weekend is Friday, right when I get home from school. From 3:00 Friday to 8:00 Monday is 65 hours of no school! School is OK, but it's nice to have a break. Plus, we have pizza and movies on Friday nights. And Mom and Dad don't make me practice my trumpet. Fridays are great!

~ Tool 4 ~

Sometimes it's hard to get writing, even with a prompt. One way to get your words flowing again is to do **FREE WRITING.** In free writing, you write whatever pops into your head. You don't have to write in sentences. You don't even have to make sense. Just keep going, without stopping. You might be surprised at what you discover.

April 3

I wonder what's for lunch today. I smell tacos but I thought tacos were on the menu for tomorrow. Yum yum yum yum I'm so hungry I could eat a horse. What a weird saying I mean who could eat a horse? Who would want to? Oh look DeVon's chewing on his pencil. I suppose I won't be able to chew on my pencil when I get my braces. Getting braces is going to be weird I wish I didn't have to get them.

~ Tool 5 ~

A journal can help with **DECISION MAKING.** You can brainstorm for ideas, then list the pros and cons of the choices you have. When you see your ideas written down, it might be easier to make up your mind. Here Riley has made a list of four gift ideas. After looking at the pros and cons, the choice seems clear.

April 5

There's a big party at Aunt Jessie's house next week.
Grandma Dee is turning 70. I need to get her a present!

IDEA	PRO	CON
school picture of me	easy to wrap	already has one
chocolate-covered cherries	her favorite treat	gave them last year
perfume	she likes it	already has a bunch
gift certificate for an afternoon of board games	we can do together	???

Gift certificate it is! Maybe include her favorite tea?
Cookies, too. The ones with the butterscotch chips.
I'll ask Mom to help.

April 9

When I grow up, I think I'd like to live in the mountains. I still remember our trip to Colorado. I was 5. Driving up Pikes Peak was so awesome. I remember seeing shadows from the clouds. The air was cold and felt kind of sharp when I breathed it in. If I lived in Colorado, maybe I could drive one of those giant snowplows in the winter. That would be great!

~ Tool 6 ~

A journal is a private place to write about your **HOPES AND DREAMS.** You might not be comfortable sharing these kinds of thoughts with your friends and family. But in your journal, your dreams are safe.

~ Tool 7 ~

In a journal, you can write whatever way you'd like. Maybe **POETRY** would express your thoughts best. Poetry comes in many forms. Try a few, and see what works best for you.

April 14

Asked Mom for a sleepover with Sam again. She told me she was tired of my begging and I had to come up with a more creative way to ask. We've been learning about acrostics in school. Maybe a poem will work with Mom. I'll try.

Sam's my best friend

Let him sleep over

Eating chips until the bag is

Empty

Please, please, please

Orange pop

Very late

Eggs and pancakes for breakfast

Repeat next weekend at Sam's house!!

April 16

Xavier taught me this drawing trick today. Pretty cool.

1. Start with a box

2. Add 4 lines

3. Add 4 more lines

4. Add 4 arcs

5. Now add 4 big arcs and connect everything together

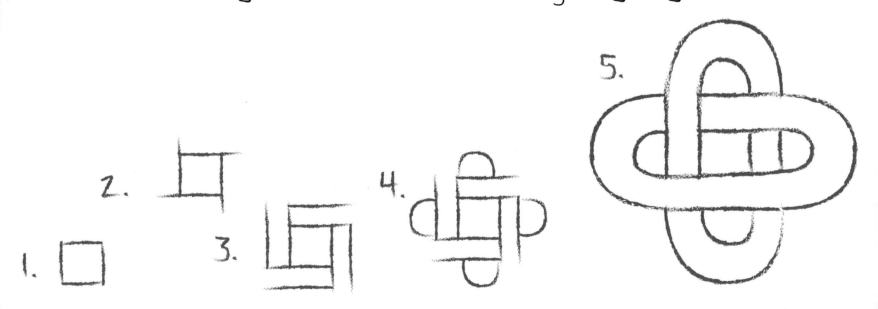

~ Tool 8 ~

Journals don't have to be just about writing. You can include **DRAWINGS**, too. They can be quick doodles, sketches, maps, or diagrams.

April 19

This is from my sleepover with Sam. I think he's still got pieces of chips in his hair.

My spelling bee trophy! I keep it in my bookcase. I won by spelling "Massachusetts."

~ Tool 9 ~

Your journal can include **KEEPSAKES** from the events you're writing about. Ticket stubs, programs, cards, photos— go ahead and tape these items into your journal. Someday you'll be glad you did.

~ Tool 10 ~

Some people like to keep journals with different **THEMES**. These journals are about the same subject. For example, you might keep a separate journal for the trips you take. You could keep one for holidays, or to record ideas for stories or poems. In addition to his everyday journal, Riley keeps a dream journal. He writes all his dreams in it.

April 22

Last night, I dreamt I was in a small room with two camels. They were standing with each leg in a bucket of water! One camel looked at me with big brown eyes. Then it slowly started stepping out of the buckets. When I woke up, I was thirsty. Weird!

One of the best things about keeping a journal is that you can see how you've changed over time. It reminds you of things you may have forgotten. A journal is a way of writing a letter to your future self.

April 23

I just found my old journal from first grade. I mixed up my d's and b's all the time and I made my q's backward. I said I wanted to walk dogs when I grew up. Maybe I can still do that in the summer. In the winter I'll be out in the snow with my snowplow, clearing the roads in Colorado!

My trip to Colorado Springs

1st Place

my blue ribbon from the science fair

my project was about how rainbows are made

Let's Review!

These are the **10 tools** you need to write a great journal.

A journal is the perfect place to record your **OBSERVATIONS (1)**. Writing down your **EMOTIONS (2)** can be like talking to a good friend.

If you get stuck and can't think of anything to write in your journal, try using **WRITING PROMPTS (3)** or **FREE WRITING (4)**.

A journal can help you with **DECISION MAKING (5)**. First brainstorm for ideas and then list their pros and cons. Seeing these lists on the pages of your journal can make the decision clear. A journal is also a safe place to record your **HOPES AND DREAMS (6)**.

Sometimes writing **POETRY (7)** might be the best way to express your thoughts. But journals don't have to be just about writing. They can include **DRAWINGS (8)** and **KEEPSAKES (9)**, too.

Some journals are about one subject or **THEME (10)**. Dreams, holidays, travel, or after-school activities could all be the subject of a theme journal.

Getting Started Exercises

- Can't think of anything to write? Try answering some of these questions: Who is your hero, and why? What famous person would you most like to meet? How would your life be different if you could fly? If you had three wishes, what would they be?

- Carry around a small notebook. When something happens that you want to write about, jot down a few reminder words. Then use those notes when you sit down to write in your journal.

- Sometimes it's easier to write if you feel like you're writing *to* someone—even if that person will never see your journal. You can write to a friend, a parent or grandparent, a teacher, or anyone else. Pretend you're talking to that person, and get writing.

- Write at the same time every day or week. That way, writing will become a good habit.

Writing Tips

 If you are writing on a computer, be sure to save your work. Back up your files often. (Ask your parents or teacher if you don't know how.) That way, if you have computer problems, you won't lose your entire journal. It's also a good idea to print it out regularly. Put the pages in a folder, or a sturdy binder.

 When you look over your journal, you might not like everything you've written. You might want to tear out some pages—but don't! Accept your journal the way it is. Your journal is a record of who you are at a certain time. Someday those pages might teach you something about yourself.

 Remember, no one is judging your journal on how well you write. Your journal is by you, for you. If you're writing a journal for class, and there's something you don't want your teacher to see, label it. Your teacher should respect your wishes.

Share a Scare

Writing Your Own Scary Story

Goosebumps and gasps. Shivers and quivers. Shudders and trembles and shakes.

Is it possible that these experiences could be *fun*?

Sure—if you're reading a scary story!

Scary stories invite us into the dark, spooky side of our imaginations. They challenge us every step of the way. At the end, we might still be scared, but we have a feeling of victory, too. Maybe that's why so many people love scary stories!

In this section, you'll learn how to write your own scary story. Start by reading our example, "The Scary-Go-Round," straight through. Then go back to page 129 and learn about the tools you can use to give your readers chills and thrills.

"Let's take that trail," Shane said.

"Let's not," argued Lila.

Lila and Shane had walked their dog at the park dozens of times. But they'd never noticed the side trail. It was a line of trampled-down grass, going up a small hill.

"I think we should go home," Lila said. "The sun is setting. It'll be dark soon."

Shane ignored her and headed up the trail.

Lila sighed. "Come on, Beans," she said to their dog.

~ Tool 1 ~

One of the first things a reader learns in a good scary story is the **SETTING**. When does the story take place? Where does it happen? Scary stories often take place in dark locations. In this story, the setting is a park at sunset.

~ Tool 2 ~

Scary stories introduce readers to at least one of the main **CHARACTERS** right away. Characters are the people or creatures in the story. The main characters are the ones who appear most often. Here we meet Shane, Lila, and their dog, Beans.

~ Tool 3 ~

SENSORY DETAILS help readers see, hear, smell, taste, and touch what's going on in the story. Here we *see* the splintered wood of the teeter-totter. We *see* the merry-go-round covered in vines and spider webs. We *hear* the rusty chains of the old swing set.

~ Tool 4 ~

FORESHADOWING is often used in scary stories. Foreshadowing gives readers hints about what might happen later in the story. Lila thinks the old playground is creepy. She's uneasy. And because she's worried, so are we.

They stopped at the top of the hill. Below them, in a clearing surrounded by trees, was an old playground.

"Cool!" Shane exclaimed.

"Creepy," Lila muttered.

They hiked down the hill until they reached a swing set made of rotting wood. The rusty chains creaked in the breeze. A splintery teeter-totter stood in a cluster of thorny bushes. Next to it was a merry-go-round covered in vines and spider webs.

"Let's go back," Lila said with a shiver.

"Oh, all right," Shane said. "I'll come back tomorrow—by myself."

~ Tool 5 ~

Together, all the events that make up a story are called the **PLOT**.

Something moved in the woods. Beans growled.

"What was *that*?" Lila asked.

"Oh, probably a giant chicken, or a two-headed fox, or—"

Shane stopped short. An old woman, her head wrapped in black, was hobbling toward them. Her skin was so wrinkly it seemed to be slipping off her face.

"Play with me?" she begged. "Play with me?"

~ Tool 6 ~

The plots of scary stories are full of **SURPRISES**. Strange, unexpected things happen. Shane and Lila (and Beans) are startled to see an old woman at the playground. Who is she? What is she doing there?

"Um, hi," Shane said nervously as Lila clutched his arm. This was too weird. What would an old lady be doing out here at sunset?

The woman seemed to read his mind. "I come here by myself all the time," she said. "I live just over there, on Willow Road."

Shane and Lila glanced at each other. There was no Willow Road. Not anymore. No one lived inside the park. Their own house was the closest one to the entrance.

~ Tool 7 ~

The mystery of the old woman deepens.
Shane and Lila don't know what to think.
Neither do we! Is the old woman simply
lost and confused? Or is there something
spooky going on? It's too soon to say.
But the **SUSPENSE** continues to build.

"Play with me?" the old woman said again. There was something odd about her eyes. Looking into them was like looking through dirty windows and seeing two small red flames. But maybe that was just the sunset reflecting in her eyes.

~ Tool 8 ~

Sometimes, writers use words to create a picture in readers' minds. This is called **IMAGERY**. The words might compare one thing to another. Here, the woman's eyes are likened to dirty windows with small flames glowing behind them. What if they had been compared to red licorice? Would you feel differently about her?

Beans tugged hard at his leash, trying to pull the kids back toward the trail.

"Don't go! Play with me!" The woman stamped her foot weakly. "Play with me!"

Lila and Shane whispered to each other, then turned back toward the woman. "Don't be upset. I'll play with you," Lila said in a polite but trembling voice. "What do you want to do?"

~ Tool 9 ~

DIALOGUE is what characters say to each other. Dialogue gives information and helps move the story along. Readers "hear" the characters talk. They feel like the story is happening right in front of them.

The woman pressed her hands together in delight. "The merry-go-round is my favorite. You go first!"

"It's not going to work," Shane whispered to Lila. "Obviously. It hasn't been used in years. And how is she going to be able to push you?"

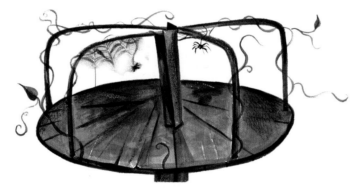

The woman heard him. "Oh, I'm a real good pusher!"

Lila shrugged helplessly at Shane. She climbed onto the merry-go-round, staying well away from the spider webs.

"Hold on tight!" the woman ordered.

Lila carefully placed her hands on a rotting woode
handle. The old woman leaned forward.

The merry-go-round creaked ... roots tore out of the ground ...
and then it slowly began to spin. The old woman let go, but the
merry-go-round kept moving. It picked up speed.

"Lila!" Shane shouted. This was too strange. They needed to get out of here. "Let's go home. NOW!"

But the merry-go-round whirred faster and faster. The old woman clapped her hands. Her eyes glowed brighter—the red flames grew bigger—

"Shane!" Lila cried. She crouched down and tried to jump off the merry-go-round. But it was going too fast. Around and around—

~ Tool 10 ~

Scary stories work best
if the main characters
TAKE ACTION. They
can't just have things
done *to* them. They need
to fight back! Shane can't
stop the merry-go-round.
But that just makes the
story more frightening.

Shane dropped Beans' leash
and ran to the merry-go-round.
He tried to put his foot on the edge and
grab the handle. But the spinning
merry-go-round threw him to the ground.

"Stop this thing!" Shane yelled at the old woman.

"You're scaring my sister!"

The woman smiled, her eyes brighter than ever. She held up a bony hand and the merry-go-round began to slow down. Slower ... and slower ... and slower.

~ Tool 11 ~

In all types of stories, **PUNCTUATION** can make a scene come alive. Exclamation points show strong feelings, such as anger or fear. Ellipses (the three dots after the word *slower*) create a pause.

The ellipses here make us feel the merry-go-round slowing down. On page 142, the dashes create a feeling of speed as the merry-go-round goes faster.

146

When the merry-go-round stopped, Lila stepped off.

"Are you all right?" Shane asked.

"Oh yes," Lila replied. "That was fun! Now it's your turn!"

She brushed the hair out of her eyes and looked straight at Shane.

147

He gasped.

~ Tool 12 ~

The **CLIMAX** is often the scariest part of a scary story. Everything that happened earlier in the story has led us to this moment.

Lila's eyes burned into his like a red flame.

~ Tool 13 ~

In most kinds of stories, the **ENDING** should leave readers satisfied. All the questions in the story have been answered. But scary stories are different. A good scary story should leave readers with their hearts pounding!

She took the old woman's hand and together they stepped toward Shane.

"Play with us!" they begged.

"Play with us!"

Let's Review!

These are the **13 tools** you need to write great scary stories.

The **SETTING** (1) of a scary story helps set the mood. The **CHARACTERS** (2) are the people or creatures in the story. **SENSORY DETAILS** (3) appeal to our five senses and help readers connect to the story.

FORESHADOWING (4) provides clues about events that will happen. Together, the events in a story make up the **PLOT (5)**. Scary stories should include **SURPRISES (6)**. **SUSPENSE (7)** builds throughout the story and keeps the reader turning pages. **IMAGERY (8)** is language that lets readers create pictures in their minds. Characters speak to each other (and give information to the reader) through **DIALOGUE (9)**. They **TAKE ACTION (10)** to solve their problems. **PUNCTUATION (11)** such as ellipses, dashes, and exclamation points can speed up or slow down the story's events.

The **CLIMAX (12)** is the peak of the story's action and is likely to be the scariest moment. The reader shouldn't feel happy or calm with the **ENDING (13)** of a scary story—the reader should feel scared!

Getting Started Exercises

- Have you ever been lost at a store, or heard a strange noise outside your window, or thought something was following you in the woods? What details do you remember? Ask your friends and family to share their scary stories. Once you get a basic idea, let your imagination take over.

- Do you remember what you dressed up as last Halloween? How about the year before that—and the year before that? Imagine those characters all together, and put them in a scary setting. What might happen?

- Dreams can be very strange, and some of them are scary. What dreams do you remember? Could any of them be used in a story?

- Scary movies often have sequels. A sequel is a story that starts where the one before it ended. Pick out a favorite scary book or movie, and see if you can keep the plot going.

Writing Tips

 Think about your five senses: seeing, hearing, touching, smelling, and tasting. Pick details that connect to those senses. You'll send shivers down your readers' spines!

 Read your story out loud—to yourself at first, and then to your friends and family. Turn out the lights and read by flashlight, to put everyone in the right mood. Pay attention to how your story sounds. Are there places that move too slowly, or too fast? Do all of your details help create a scary feeling?

 Remember that there are lots of types of scary stories. Some have the traditional scary characters and settings—ghosts, haunted houses, and so on. Other scary stories are more like real life. What matters is that, in the end, the reader is spooked!

JUST THE FACTS

Writing Your Own Research Report

AUSTRALIA

A research report is a special kind of writing assignment. You don't tell a story. You don't make things up. In fact, writing is one of the LAST steps in putting together a research report.

First you'll need to pick a topic. You'll learn what experts have to say about your topic. You'll take notes. You'll organize facts. And when you're done with those steps? THEN you'll write.

Writing a research report is a challenging task—but a fun one, too. By the time you've finished your report, you'll be a mini expert yourself!

polar bear—is losing its home because of global warming

vampire bat—drinks blood!

platypus—has a weird bill, lays eggs

koala—cute!

python—up to 33 feet long, and can swallow a goat!

~ Tool 1 ~

Every research report starts with a **TOPIC**. Pick one that interests you. The more interested you are, the more fun it will be. Make a list of possible ideas. Then start narrowing it down. Look up a few quick facts, if you're not sure about your choices.

~ Tool 2 ~

The research begins! Books, magazines, and newspapers are good **SOURCES** of information. So is the Internet. You might even talk to a person who is an expert on your topic.

If you use the Internet, make sure your sources are trustworthy. Look for well-known Web sites. If you're not sure, ask your teacher or librarian.

Try for at least three sources. If a book or article is too difficult (or too easy), put it aside and try to find something more fitting. Don't worry about your report the first time you read your sources. Just enjoy learning about your subject.

Where do platypuses live?

What do platypuses look like?

Do platypuses have any enemies?

What do platypuses eat?

~ Tool 3 ~

Once you're familiar with your topic, start **BRAINSTORMING.** Write down all the questions you might want to answer in your report. You probably won't be able to include everything in your report, but that's OK.

Do female platypuses really lay eggs?

How many eggs do they lay?

How long do platypuses live?

Are platypuses endangered?

What sounds do platypuses make?

How big is a platypus?

Do platypuses swim? Do they walk?

Are platypuses active in the day or night?

~ Tool 4 ~

The next step in writing a research report is to take **NOTES.** Index cards make note-taking easier. Write one of your brainstorming questions at the top of each card. As you re-read your sources, record the answers to your questions on the cards. You might need more than one card per question.

Include the name of your sources on your index cards, as well as page numbers or Web site addresses. If any questions come up later, you'll know exactly where to look.

Where do platypuses live?

Tasmania and Eastern Australia—<u>Platypus!</u>, page 10

beside streams, rivers, and lakes in eastern and southeastern Australia, stretching from Queensland down to Victoria and Tasmania—<u>A Platypus' World</u>, pages 3, 22

What do platypuses eat?

insects, larvae, shellfish, and worms—nationalgeographic.com

worms, insects, fish eggs, water plants, shrimp—<u>A Platypus' World</u>, pages 3, 6

Introduction (riddle)

Where the platypus lives, how big it is

The snout

The tail

The feet

How the female lays eggs

Baby platypuses

Conclusion

~ Tool 5 ~

Writing your report will be easier if you plan ahead. An **OUTLINE** will help you do this. An outline lists the ideas of a report, in the order they will be presented.

Some outlines are very simple. The example here on the left is a simple outline. It lists general ideas rather than specific facts. Other outlines are detailed, like the one on the right. Use the type of outline that works best for you.

Introduction

riddle: What has a bill like a duck, a tail like a beaver,
and feet like an otter?
- not a joke
- strange mammal but actually makes sense

habitat, appearance
- lives near lakes and streams in Australia and Tasmania
- about half the size of a cat
- brown, waterproof fur
- active mostly at night

snout
- dark rubbery skin, tiny holes with nerve endings
- nerves sense motion, help find food
- uses bill to dig up food
- eats worms, insects, shrimp, fish eggs

tail
- flat and wide, like a beaver's but is covered with fur
- uses tail and hind legs to steer while swimming
- uses tail to carry away dirt from digging

QUACK!

+

You've picked your topic. You've done your research, taken notes, and made an outline. It's time to write!

What has a bill like a duck, a tail like a beaver, and feet like an otter? This question sounds like a joke. But it's not. The answer is: a platypus! The platypus is one of the strangest mammals on our planet. But when we take a close look, we can see that this odd animal makes sense.

~ Tool 6 ~

The first paragraph in a research report is the **INTRODUCTION.** The introduction should do two things. It should get the reader's attention in some way. And it should state what the report will be about.

This introduction begins like a riddle. It "hooks" us. We know that the platypus is different from other mammals. And we want to keep reading, to find out why.

mammals on our planet. But when we take a closer look, we can see that this odd animal makes sense.

Platypuses live near lakes and streams in eastern Australia and the island of Tasmania. They are about half the size of a cat. They have brown, waterproof fur. They are active mostly at night.

platypus habitat

Australia

Tasmania

~ Tool 7 ~

The **BODY** is the main part of a research report. It is usually three or more paragraphs. The body includes the most important information about the topic.

It's a good idea to provide some basic information early in your report. In this paragraph, we find out where platypuses live. We find out how big they are, too. If we didn't learn those things right away, we might wonder about them throughout the report.

at night.

The most unusual part of a platypus is its bill, or snout. The bill is covered with dark rubbery skin. It has tiny holes all over it. Inside the holes are nerve endings. These nerves sense motion. They help the platypus find its food. Platypuses use their bills to dig up food from the mud. They eat shrimp, worms, fish eggs, and insects.

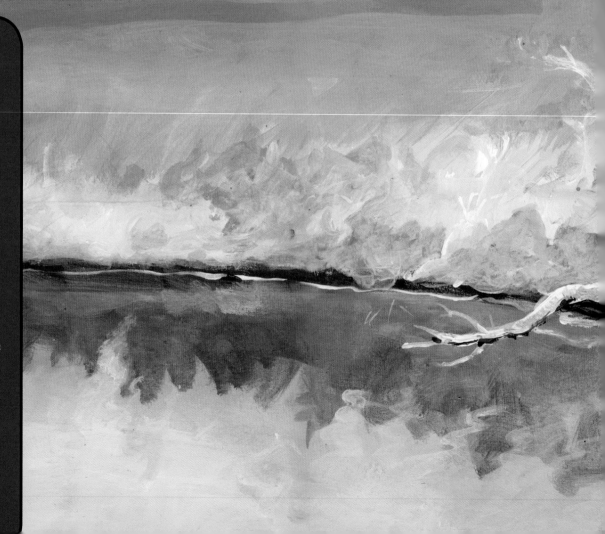

~ Tool 8 ~

The first sentence in a paragraph is called a **TOPIC SENTENCE.** It lets the reader know what will be talked about in that paragraph. It's like a mini introduction. After the topic sentence, every sentence that follows should add detail. Here the topic sentence introduces us to the platypus' bill.

the holes are nerve endings. These nerves sense motion. They help the platypus find its food. Platypuses use their bills to dig up food from the mud. They eat shrimp, worms, fish eggs, and insects.

The platypus has a flat, wide tail. It's shaped like a beaver's tail. The tail is covered with fur. The platypus uses its tail and hind legs to steer while swimming. The platypus also uses its tail to carry away dirt when digging a burrow. Fat is stored in the tail, too. The fat gives the platypus extra energy during the winter months, when there is less food.

Like otters, platypuses have webbed feet. The platypus' front feet are like paddles. They help the platypus swim. On land, the webbing folds up between the platypus' claws. The platypus' short legs are on the side of its body. The platypus is a good swimmer, but a slow walker.

As you write your report, remember what you promised your reader in the introduction. Do your best to stay on track.

So far we have learned how the platypus uses its strange tail, feet, and bill. We see that the platypus does indeed make sense.

~ Tool 9 ~

SENTENCE VARIETY

makes a report more interesting to read. Start your sentences in different ways. Sentences often begin with nouns ("The platypus") or pronouns ("She," "He," "It," or "They"). That's fine. Just don't start *all* your sentences that way. See how the third and fourth sentences in the first paragraph are different from the rest? That's an example of sentence variety.

but a slow walker.

This mammal has another very strange feature. It lays eggs! In spring, the female makes a long tunnel with a burrow at the end. Using her tail, she brings in leaves and reeds to line her burrow. She lays one to three small, leathery eggs. She keeps the eggs warm for about 10 days.

When the baby platypuses hatch, they are blind and hairless. They are called "puggles." They drink milk through tiny holes in the mother's skin. The puggles are fed by their mother for about four months. Then they leave the burrow and start learning how to catch their own food.

~ Tool 10 ~

The last paragraph in a research report is the **CONCLUSION.** Remind the reader of your main points. If possible, go back to an idea in your introduction. Bring your report to a pleasing close.

When the platypus was first seen by Europeans in 1798, people thought it was a prank. They couldn't believe that the creature was real. But now we know better. The platypus might look strange, but its bill helps it find and catch food. Its tail and webbed feet help it to swim and dig burrows. The platypus is no joke!

~ Tool 11 ~

REVISION is an important part of all good writing. Pretend you're reading your report for the very first time. Are your facts presented in an order that makes sense? Are you missing any important facts? Or have you included facts that aren't needed? You might need to cut, add, or move information.

~ Tool 12 ~

When you're happy with how your report is put together, it's time to **PROOFREAD**. Check your spelling. Make sure your commas, periods, and other punctuation are used correctly.

~ Tool 13 ~

The final step in writing a research report is a **BIBLIOGRAPHY.** A bibliography lets the reader know where you got your information. Bibliographies can be written in many different styles. Ask your teacher for help, or you can follow the example on page 181.

BIBLIOGRAPHY

BOOKS

author name

book title

publisher location

Arnold, Caroline. *A Platypus' World.* Minneapolis: Picture Window Books, 2008.

publisher name

publication year

Clarke, Ginjer L. *Platypus!* New York: Random House, 2004.

Note: You can find this information on the copyright page of a book. The page is usually in the beginning of a book. It includes the copyright symbol ©. For an example, look at the copyright page of this book.

WEB SITES

Web site name

date article viewed

"Platypus Profile." National Geographic. 13 Jan 2009. <http://animals.nationalgeographic.com/animals/mammals/platypus.html>

article name

Web site address (URL)

Let's Review!

These are the **13 tools** you need to write great research reports.

Every research report starts with a **TOPIC (1)**. Then the research begins. Good **SOURCES (2)** of information include books, magazines, and Web sites. **BRAINSTORMING (3)** helps the writer decide what information to include in the report. **NOTES (4)** and an **OUTLINE (5)** help organize the report and make writing easier.

The **INTRODUCTION (6)** lets readers know what the report is about. The **BODY (7)** contains most of the information. Every paragraph in the body should start with a **TOPIC SENTENCE (8)**. Starting sentences in different ways creates **SENTENCE VARIETY (9)** and makes the report more interesting to read. The last paragraph is the **CONCLUSION (10)**. It sums up the report and brings it to an end.

The **REVISION (11)** step allows the writer to add, cut, or move facts around. In the **PROOFREADING (12)** step, the writer takes a close look at spelling, punctuation, and grammar. The final part of the research report is the **BIBLIOGRAPHY (13)**. It lists the sources used to write the report.

Getting Started Exercises

- Writing a good research report takes time. To keep yourself on track, use a calendar. Give yourself deadlines for finding sources, writing an outline, finishing your first draft, and so on. That way, you can do your best work with every step. You won't feel rushed at the last minute.

- Are you having trouble picking a topic? Think about your favorite books, movies, and TV shows. Think about trips you've taken with your family. Ask people who their heroes are. If you do these things, you'll probably find a topic in no time. For example, maybe one of your favorite movies is about penguins. You could write a report on penguins, or about Antarctica. Or maybe your grandfather loves the music of Elvis Presley. Elvis would be a good topic.

- Chances are, your older siblings or friends have written research reports for school. Ask them if they have any advice. And if you run into trouble while you're writing your report, you can ask them for help, too.

Writing Tips

When you take notes, don't copy from your sources word for word. Just write down a few key words. That way, when you start writing, you'll sound like yourself.

Sometimes the facts you find in one source will be different from the facts in another source. Ask your parents, teacher, or librarian which source is the best to use. If they don't know, go ahead and pick one source as your main one. Be consistent in using that source. For example, if you get an animal's weight from one source, get its length from that source, too.

Ask a friend, sibling, or parent to look over your report. They might see mistakes that you missed.

Put your finished report in a folder or sheet protector. That way, when you hand it in, it will be clean and unwrinkled.

Glossary

acrostic—a poem in which the first letters of each line spell out a word or phrase

alliteration—using several words that start with the same letter sound

bibliography—a list of books, articles, and other sources that are used in the writing of a paper; the bibliography is placed at the end of the paper

body—the main part of a letter or other written piece

brainstorming—to come up with lots of ideas all at once, without stopping to judge them

character—a person, animal, or creature in a story

cinquain—a five-line poem that follows a 2-4-6-8-2 pattern of syllables

climax—a story's most exciting moment

closing—the end of a letter

communicate—to pass along thoughts, feelings or information

compare—to look closely at things in order to discover ways they are alike or different

conclusion—the final part of a written piece

concrete poem—a poem that takes the shape of its subject

consistent—to do something the same way every time

cordially—friendly, warmly

culture—a nation or group of people with shared beliefs and customs

decision—the result of making up your mind about something

delight—great enjoyment or pleasure

detail—one of many facts about a certain thing or a small part of a larger thing

dialogue—the words spoken between two or more characters; in writing, dialogue is set off with quotation marks

emotions—feelings

ending—the last of three main story parts; the finish

expert—someone who knows a lot about a certain topic

express—to say or show

foreshadowing—giving hints about what might happen in the future

formal—official and proper

free verse poem—a type of poem that follows no form or subject rules

free writing—writing whatever pops into your head, without stopping

grammar—rules about using words

greed—wanting more of something than is actually needed

greeting—the beginning of a letter

haiku—a three-line poem that follows a 5-7-5 pattern of syllables

heading—the part of a letter that includes the writer's and reader's addresses and the date

imagery—words used to create pictures in readers' minds

index card—a small card made of heavy paper, used for taking notes

introduction—the first part of a written piece

journal—a written record of thoughts, feelings, and experiences

keepsake—an object that reminds us of a person or event

limerick—a silly five-line poem in which the first two lines rhyme with the last, and the third and fourth lines rhyme with each other

magic—the power to control things with charms or spells

metaphor—a figure of speech that compares different things without using words such as *like* or *as*

mistake—something done incorrectly

notes—bits of written information

observations—things that we notice or study

onomatopoeia—words that copy the sound they are describing, such as *hiss*

outline—the main points of a written piece, in the order they appear

plot—what happens in a story

postscript—a message or note added after the writer's signature; *P.S.* stands for "postscript"

problem-solving—finding answers to things that cause trouble

program—a paper that lists the order of events in a performance, such as a band concert or play

proofread—to read to find and fix mistakes

pros and cons—reasons for (pros) and against (cons) doing something

punctuation—marks used to make written language clear; examples include periods, commas, and question marks

regards—to show respect

repetition—doing, saying, or making something again and again

research—to study a subject in an organized way

revise, revision—to change something; to "re-vision" it, or see it in a new way or make it better

rhyme—word endings that sound the same

rhythm—a pattern of beats, like in music

secret—information known only to oneself or a few people

sensory—having to do with the five senses: sight, smell, hearing, taste, and touch

setting—the time and place of a story

signature—the writer's handwritten name

signature line—the writer's typed name below his or her handwritten signature

simile—a figure of speech that compares different things using words such as *like* or *as*

source—a book, article, person, or group that provides information about a topic

suspense—worry, unease

syllable—a small unit of language that includes a vowel sound; a syllable is like a beat in music

theme—the main idea of something

topic—a subject or main area of interest

topic sentence—the first sentence in a paragraph that tells what the paragraph will be about

trampled—to be walked on many times, crushed

tricks—actions done to fool people

variety—a group of things that are different from each other

whir—to spin very fast

wicked—evil, bad, wrong

Index

About the Author

Nancy Loewen has published nearly 100 nonfiction books for children on a variety of topics, including bugs, planets, grammar, and citizenship. Her books have received awards from the American Library Association, the New York Public Library, and Parents' Choice. Her book *Four to the Pole!*, co-authored with Ann Bancroft, was nominated for a Minnesota Book Award.

Nancy has a B.A. in English and an M.F.A. in creative writing. She lives in Minnesota with her husband, two children, two cats, a chubby beagle, and an even chubbier guinea pig, who likes to nibble on her toes while she writes.

About th

Christopher Lyles is a professional illustrator who spends much of his time working in a variety of media and exploring new fields. Since graduating from art school in 2001, he has contributed to children's publications, greeting cards, editorial illustrations, and gallery installations.

Chris' illustrations have been recognized by The Society of Illustrators LA and American Illustration. Chris also exhibits his work on the East Coast and in Los Angeles.

Living in the small town of Simsbury, Connecticut, with his wife and their dog, Riley, Chris enjoys hiking, exercising, traveling, teaching art to children, and looking for old stuff.

Illustrators

Dawn Beacon is an illustrator living in Vail, Colorado. She has worked as a designer and illustrator for local newspapers, print companies, and various non-profits.

Visit her art at www.dawnbeacon.com.

Todd Ouren has been a professional artist for more than 20 years. He has illustrated and designed numerous award-winning books and greeting cards. Raised near Fergus Falls, Minnesota, Todd now lives in Mankato, Minnesota, with his wife and three boys. In his spare time, he enjoys watching his kids play sports, traveling, hiking, kayaking, and spending time at the lake.

Editor: Jill Kalz
Designer: Abbey Fitzgerald
Page Production: Melissa Kes
Art Director: Nathan Gassman
Editorial Director: Nick Healy
Creative Director: Joe Ewest
The illustrations in this book were created with acrylics, acrylic and collage, or digitally.

Picture Window Books
1710 Roe Crest Drive
North Mankato, MN 56003
www.capstonepub.com

Library of Congress Cataloging-in-Publication Data
Loewen, Nancy.
Writer's toolbox : learn how to write letters, fairy tales, scary stories, journals, poems, and reports / by Nancy Loewen ; illustrated by Christopher Lyles, Todd Ouren, and Dawn Beacon. — Minneapolis, MN : Picture Window Books, 2010.
192 p. : col. ill. ; cm.
Includes index and glossary.
Includes bibliographic references.
ISBN 978-1-4048-5905-0 (paperback)
1. Authorship — Juvenile literature. 2. Creative writing — Juvenile literature.

Printed in the United States   4584